Lowcountry Lost

and other poems for everyday life

Moultrie Townsend

Lowcountry Lost
and other poems for everyday life

Copyright © 2024 by Moultrie Townsend

ISBNs:
979-8-9914275-0-0 (paperback)
979-8-9914275-1-7 (eBook)

Rememberances

Sailor and Friend

Sailor, doctor and friend.
Southern gentleman to the end.
Haha to some, Doc to all.
Happy to weed the garden or throw the ball.

A traveler and a homebody.
Been known to enjoy a beer.
A wry sense of humor
Reserved for moments when others would cheer.

A sense of history
Hidden in his very name.
I consider myself privileged
To share in the same.

So I thank him for all that he was and all that he's done.
It was a wild ride but so much fun.
I must always remember and never forget
The lessons he taught, even the ones I haven't caught just yet.

Now all we can do is laugh to keep from crying.
I guess it's what comes with dying.
Hold on too tight and you'll lose it,
So I gently let him go bit by bit.

Ebb Tide

Lost are old forts through the big oak tree.
I still remember s'mores by the old oyster cooker.
So little but still just me.
Papa so alive then- his laugh like the sun
Beaming rays of light down to you and me.
Seconds pass, and you'll see
Those adolescent years still a bit hazy.
Cutthroat games until midnight.
A precarious truce between John and me.
Time does not take the core out of Rockville.
From Saida to little Saida,
The youthful exuberance of arriving
Is as fresh as the last afternoon there.
Azaleas in full bloom.
Party lights and fireworks as far as the eye can see.
How many regattas did this place experience?
A place always covered in salt water, plough mud and sand.
On a good day, the creek yielded a few stone crabs to split
    all around.

Happy memories under the tree overlooking the bluff.
Even as the old dock sinks back into the sea.
Memories thick as the soup cooked special for the
    February nights
When the furnace heaters wouldn't light.
The place wasn't built to be a luxury resort,
But rather as a resting place for two of the sweetest souls
    Rockville has ever known.
Joy in the using and pain in the leaving.
How many boats have been trailered out of there
And how many fish have proudly been brought back in.
A tear shed for the last part of Rockville
And a wish that it may be enjoyed by others for decades
    to come.

Goodbye Beer Garden

Mulch and memories
Lie beside the wooden table
Shaped like a sewing spool.
Watch out for splinters if you're able

To scooch up to see the bandstand
And the view of the river.
No music anymore,
And the déjà vu makes me shiver.

Beer no longer flows,
And revelers no longer gorge.
No more chance meetings or long-lost reunions,
But lasting friendships here were forged.

This place will always remind me
As long as I live in this tiny town
Of golf carts, music and friendly dogs
And the best beer and cheer around.

Friend's House

Pretty pink azaleas by the front porch.
White stucco like no one builds anymore.
Patchy grass feels like country to me,
But the broken asphalt leads to the inner-city store.

The back yard's an oasis.
A wonderland for relaxation and play.
Trees and shrubbery so well cared for.
A fire pit perhaps for a colder day.

Two cars in the driveway.
Two bikes tucked 'round back.
This place was meant for living.
Just the space to get your life on track.

Inside, such happiness and joy.
Smells of coffee and pie fill the air.
Friends and family come freely through that door,
And once inside, you'll feel at home forevermore.

Porch Party

Ten minutes on the porch.
Lightning flashes just beyond the trees.
Conversations unabated.
Rain starts to patter on the leaves.

Wine flows, and songs are played.
The rain comes down in sheets.
There's a peaceful feeling together here.
A more cheerful bunch you'll rarely meet.

Then, as night turns to morning,
The rain's still coming in sideways.
A few more songs and then we're done
To go our separate ways.

Our host is understandably nervous
As the road is slick to get back home,
But what a wet and wonderful evening of music we had
With a finale: "Kodachrome"

A Full Day

Hammocks hang gracefully under Spanish moss,
As you sip your lemonade sweet as the summer air.
Poolside someone's beckoning you to join in the fray.
Marco Polo shouted in a silly voice for all to hear.

Boiled peanuts cooking and watermelon sliced.
Shrimp and corn turning on the grill.
Stuffed and nursing just one more beer.
A plan for the evening is just becoming clear.

A boat ride in search of dolphins sounds mighty grand.
The sea air will wash all this chlorine away.
Hurling toward infinity with country tunes on.
The boat is really humming today.

Back to the dock for a few hours more
Of music and old stories, to us never bore.
An old movie plays in the background as we drift off to sleep.
Feeling on top in a life now complete.

Rockville

Rockville. Down a windy dirt road with a few limbs in the way.

Rockville. A worn fire pit shoots sparks at the tall trees above.

Rockville. A floating dock sits in the mud looking out over the marsh to the river.

Rockville. Hours of cutthroat on the deck until bedtime.

Rockville. Generations of forts and games of capture the flag.

Ebb Tide. It was our little corner of Rockville, SC.

It was literally the last sliver of land in the recently incorporated town,

But to us, it was an entire world and above all the penultimate destination.

Lowcountry Lost

Oyster shells and crab buckets
Line my memories
Trapped inside this place so loosely
To extend my misery.

The shrimp boats go out without me:
Jenny May and Betty Sue.
Sunsets ring so hollow
Apart from the ocean blue.

Beaches

Beach Walk

Ocean waves tumble in softly
At dawn at the beach
Where the sea birds scurry,
Making tracks just beyond the reach

Of the falling tide we encounter
On our walk just beyond the dunes.
The air so rejuvenating.
The waves blocked out by my morning tunes.

Our feet set the imprint
Up and down the beach line.
The salt leaps up in our hair
And bits of sand so very fine

Line our shoes and must be washed out
When at long last we return
From our visit to the ocean's edge
From which we still have so much to learn.

Beach Chairs

Easing into beach chairs,
Your drink spills with delight
Of an afternoon with friends spent
Singing songs that ease the height

Of a week of mounting troubles
Too momentous to comprehend.
All together, your laughter renders
Your ills forever on the mend.

Each week in season, y'all return to the place
Where it happens all again.
The week's woes sandwiched between
The company of friends.

Beach rain

Wind gusts cascade down the beach
Carrying with them a towel and a sheet
Giving us pause to carry on at our spot
So carefully selected that morning to beat the heat.

Cracking open a soda, we elect to stay a while
And catch a glimpse of a rain cloud to the far right.
That prickly feeling of anticipation comes over us
That often precedes the horizon's shift from day to night.

The next real gust seals our fate,
And our focus shifts to gathering our things in a rush.
Luckily, the wind stays at our backs
As we proceed back to the house.

Almost there, the rain starts to encircle us.
Once inside, another beach day is in the books.
As we sip our lemonade, one of us starts to grin
As the dogs greet us with happy looks.

The storm rages on for an hour or two.
Naps are taken, and shows are put on to entertain,
But I just sit on the covered porch
To take in the rhythm of the splendid beach rain.
All the frenzy of the day
Quickly melts down and washes away.

Beach Fire

Black rocks along the shore
Lead back to the beach fire
Blazing all night long.
Easing into a state that doesn't tire.

Faces blend into the opposing landscape.
Songs ring out with requisite cheer.
The sand beneath my toes shifts swiftly,
As I rise slowly to grab a beer.

Another log goes on as sparks fly ever higher.
A night like this can only lead to desire
To live life like this every day.
All I have right now is a memory pictured this way.

View from the shore

The mast towers with the sail slightly flapping.
Smoke billows from the top of the ship passing by.
Nearly missing each other, worlds away,
As the floating city starts to black out the vision of match-
sticks floating on air.

The passengers sip on cocktails hanging over the rail.
The sailors down cervezas on their way back from a fading
sunset.
Artificial light gleams off the water,
And a navigation light blinks from the sailboat heading
due north.

Both are heading home.
Each in their own way.
For the sailors, the marina's not too far away,
And for the cruisers, they'll be in Miami in about a day.

We sip on our drinks in our chairs by the shore
Witnessing this scene play out like so many times before.
As the light fades into darkness, we take a moment to pause,
And toast to the sailors and travelers out there on the horizon
until they completely fade away.

Long weekend at the beach

The wind whistles through the sea pines.
A distant call through the porch screen announces
Suppertime to the beachgoers
Who stumble home sopping wet.

A folding wagon stuffed with beach toys
Chronicles all the fun had that day,
And the beach chairs out at twilight
Put their leisure on display.

Three days and nights like this
Does a long weekend make
In the majestic, indented corners of the Carolina coast
Where the spoils of town life are theirs to take.

Lowcountry Summer

Stepping out into the heat in flip-flops.
Sunshine perfects my day.
Baseball's on the tv,
But who really knows the score?
Fishing off the pier is fine.
We don't have to be in 'til ten.
The beach calls us toward the ocean deep.
Beat by the waves until we creep
Back to the house where on the balcony
We are to see fireworks on display,
But nature, she has other plans,
As a thunderstorm comes our way.
Lightning dances in the distance
Off where the boats beat against the shore,
But our vacation's not really ruined
Just 'cuz God showed up at our door.

Mountains

Mountain Church Camp

Lightning bugs in summer
Provide the nite-lite for my mountain slumber.
Meditation at twilight
Generates magic in the air.
Light-weight vests are donned 'til sunlight
Peeks over the mountain to the valley down below.
Lightening the weight of the world.
This plush green hideout feeds the soul.
Light reflects off the cross overlooking the lake
Where vacationers come to play.
In the evening, kids share the limelight.
A talent show's the pinnacle of a lovely stay.

Visiting Autumn

The colors swirl from the mountaintop,
As a vista view is worth a stop.
Appalachia reached, and my ears just pop.

The rivers rush, and the creek nearby
Proves inviting only to fishing guides.
A light jacket rests by my side.

Passing school buses on the overpass,
We feel as though we've trespassed
On a season built for the strong and steadfast.

The light begins to fade sooner that we had planned,
And we speed back toward more Southern land
Where the chill falls softer upon the sand.

Morning Walk

Pebbles and butterflies
By the river winding.
Up ahead, a field fresh with dew.
Every morning, an adventure tried and true.
Deer along the path last Tuesday.
A black snake two weeks past.
These memories dot the landscape
That make morning's serene views last.

Kanuga's Mountain Mist

Early morning mist off the lake
Fills my mind with dreams
Of the happiest times these mountains have seen.
Every year it seems

The tea just tastes sweeter,
And the balloons soar their highest yet.
Nothing holds us back
But this moment of regret

That all in our lives aren't here to partake
In this moment of purest bliss.
Capture these memories in your mind,
All emblazoned- not to be missed.

Autumn Overlook

Swirling like the finest sherbet
On a crisp, autumn day.
The colors of the leaves mesmerize
Causing me to stay
For a minute more on this overlook
Under a sky so crystal clear.
So fine I can almost taste the beauty
That abounds this time of year.

November Party

Darkness descends,
As a chill fill the air.
Music flows playfully
Through the trees over there,
Already losing their leaves
As we string up the lights.
Holidays await us
In such a fine flight
Of fancy that seems just a moment away.
Just now remembering to soak up every day.
The feast day is not all the month has in store,
So let down your hair to party once more.

Mountain Rain

The rain trickles down the latticework.
The brick is slick to the touch.
The overhang protects us in this state
Of relaxation- not missing too much.

The distant mountain belches smoke:
Dew and mist through air so pure.
An adventure through the valley awaits us,
But this bath will first all but cure

The ills that plagued our yesterdays
And sorrows too numerous to count.
Alas, the sun just peaks out,
And a new journey begins, free of doubt.

Sundries

My Nephew's High School Graduation Poem

Watching fireflies in the mountains.
Holding you in my arms.
Seeing the world through your eyes
Gave me a glimpse of who you'd come to be.

You were filled with a sense of wonder,
And now always seeking a bigger prize.
From the court to the field,
Your drive never failed to surprise

The doubters who you left behind.
You are always confident in your mission.
From the court to the classroom,
You're always in position

To take the next step
To at last claim your prize,
As you step out into the world
With a pure heart and open eyes.

I believe you are bound for greatness,
And indeed have already won,
As you have all the pillars
To build your life upon.

Off to look for Rossiya

Chinese in the train station clutching to their visas.
Uzbekis in the market peddling their wares.
Chechens in souped-up cars as if they're in a gang.
New Russians flying private jets to Switzerland.
Old women collecting cans just to get by.
Buryat Mongols heading back to the Buddhist monastery.
Chukchis collecting driftwood in the snow.
Tatars off to the mosque for prayer.
Georgians opening up a barbeque joint for all to feast,
And on top of it all sits the new czar.
It's really more of an idea than a country.

Contrast

In a Charleston summer
Strolling along the Palmetto-lined battery,
Two children dressed in summer whites
And blues are pulled along in their red wheelbarrow
By their hippie nouveau rich mother.
In a Russian winter,
Trudging along the snow-covered path between
The apartment building and the factory
Two children, covered in many layers of
Winter clothing, are pulled along on
Their simple wooden sled by their
Poor, long-suffering mother.
Should these two worlds ever meet,
Children's laughter would be the only common language.

Tourist

The yellow-checkered chariot
Carries me back in time
To where arches commemorate victories long ago
Forgotten, but they still guard the place.
Where architecture seeps out into the townfolk's blood.
Careless and free on this sun-drenched day.
Cool breezes drift in from the mountains far away.
Standing beautiful and menacing,
Steeped in old folklore.
The trip will all be worth it
If I reach the top before
The next train back to my base,
Back from where I came.
I will always remember that smell of rubber
Mixed with the impending mountain rain.

Homeless Moment

Brush forms the outline of a hobo's trail.
The distant sunset might not avail
His hope of a home soon found.
Desperately hoping that there's no train bearing down
On his soul, so fragile at first glance,
But two days ago did do a dance.
In the midst of beauty, nothing's sure.
Stop and think to drink in what's pure.

Beside an Abandoned Building

Shadows on a winter day
Spread across the graffitied wall.
Desolate corner of the city.
Backs to the world, they stand so tall.

Branches dance in their scene.
The horizon hazy but still there.
Time stands still for this band of wise men.
Content now to just stand and stare.

Kept

Like a xylophone solo
In a rock n' roll band.
One whispers softly
When one most needs a hand,
Because the cry that won't go down
Into chapter and verse
Is the hidden dimension
That's you unrehearsed.

Politics

Tentacles spreading toxins on the body politic.
Never at a loss for dirty tricks.
Still ordinary people are all but sure
That our mission remains good and pure.
The evil changes faces over time,
And war for us is not a crime.
Empire carries a heavy weight,
And business leaves with every freighter
That carries our ideas across the shores.
Still it leaves our people wanting more.
A vote approaches, and no one can unite.
A choice is proposed,
But our motivation is fright
That our leaders are idiots, and the system isn't fair.
What it all boils down to is I no longer care.
Just leave me alone with your robocall,
And let this year pass with no fall at all.

www.ingramcontent.com/pod-product-compliance
Lightning Source LLC
Chambersburg PA
CBHW060358130626
46553CB00003B/1281